First published by Secret Quay Media Inc. 2015

Copyright © M. Gail Daldy 2013 - 2018

All rights reserved. No part of this publication may be reproduced in any form or means, graphic, electronic, or mechanical without the prior written permission of the publisher.

Things That Happen By Chance
Dyslexia Edition | http://dyslexicfonts.com

ISBN 978-0-9947957-6-2

Learn By Chance book series:
To order a copy of the book email *orders@learnbychancebooks.com*, or call 1-604-947-9283

Visit us online at www.learnbychancebooks.com

Creative Director:
Jason Bamford | Bamford Design | www.bamforddesign.com

Photographs by Gail Daldy

A special thank you to Mark Johnston for all his help.

Published By:
Secret Quay Media Inc.
Box 91194
West Vancouver, British Columbia, Canada
V7V 3N6

www.secretquaymedia.com

Printed in USA

OpenDyslexic is an open source font created to increase readability and assist with some of the common challenges faced by readers with dyslexia. The bottoms of the letters are weighted heavier to indicate direction, making it easier to quickly identify which part of the letter is down. It also aids in recognizing the correct letter and sometimes helps to keep your brain from wanting to rotate them. Consistently weighted bottoms can also assist in reinforcing the line of text. The unique shapes of each letter can help prevent the confusion through flipping and swapping.

OpenDyslexic is being continuously updated and improved based on input from other dyslexic users. If the use of the OpenDyslexic font is helpful to even some children learning to read, then I feel it is well worth including it in this edition of "Things That Happen By Chance".
http://dyslexicfonts.com

What Happened By Chance

While looking through some photographs of our son Chance growing up they instantly took me back in time to his early childhood. As my gift to him upon graduating high school I thought it would be fun to put together a collection of these chance snapshots into a little book.

The type face is actually created from some of his earliest hand writing in primary school. My hope was that he would be able to reflect back on his childhood and some of the special moments and share these everyday life lessons that he had learned as a child with his own children. It was these moments after all that made him into the person he has grown up to be.

Hopefully you can enjoy the book with your own little readers and with a smile talk about the simple things in life that teach them so much.

A Special Thanks - I'd like to thank my parents for making me aware of these little things in life.

www.learnbychancebooks.com

To Chance:

For affording me a mother's ultimate pleasure of watching you become *you.*

Things That Happen By Chance

Sharing simple life lessons with children everywhere

Life is always filled with little surprises

Life is always filled with little surprises

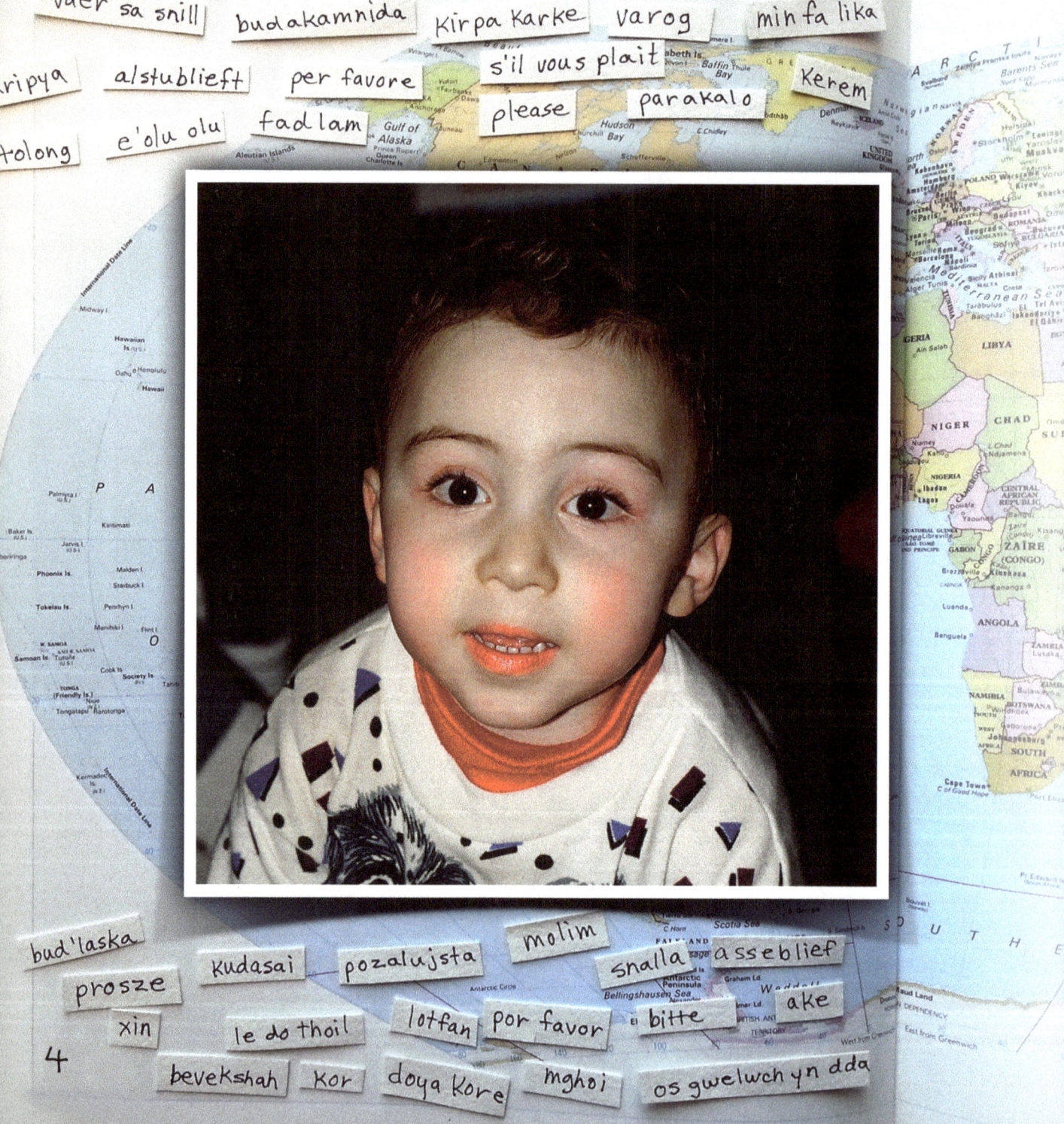

When you are asking for something always remember to say please

When you are asking for something always remember to say please

When someone helps you
always remember to smile
and say thank you

When someone helps you
always remember to smile
and say thank you

If you chew gum
remember 3 things :
1. Keep it in your mouth
2. Don't swallow it
3. Never put it in your hair

If you chew gum
remember 3 things :
1. Keep it in your mouth
2. Don't swallow it
3. Never put it in your hair

When there is a job to be done it helps to plan your attack

When there is a job to be done it helps to plan your attack

And stick to it

And stick to it

Until the very end

Until the very end

No
I don't think I ate
any cheesies

No
I don't think I ate
any cheesies

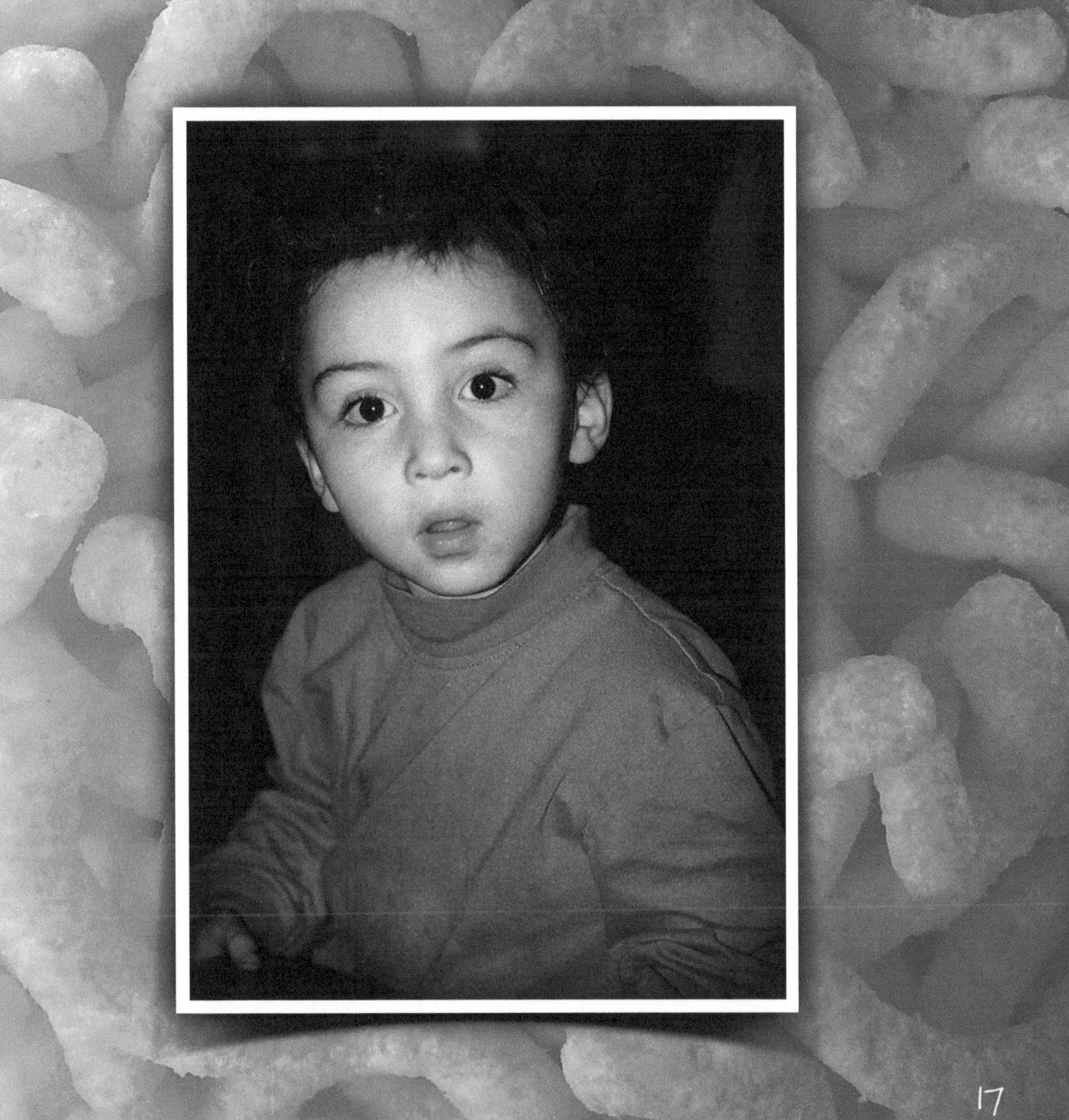

Feeding the
birds and ducks
is lots of fun

Feeding the
birds and ducks
is lots of fun

But don't forget
to close
the gate

But don't forget
to close
the gate

You can eat
too much
chocolate cake

You can eat
too much
chocolate cake

Be sure to brush your teeth every day to keep them clean and healthy

Be sure to brush your teeth every day to keep them clean and healthy

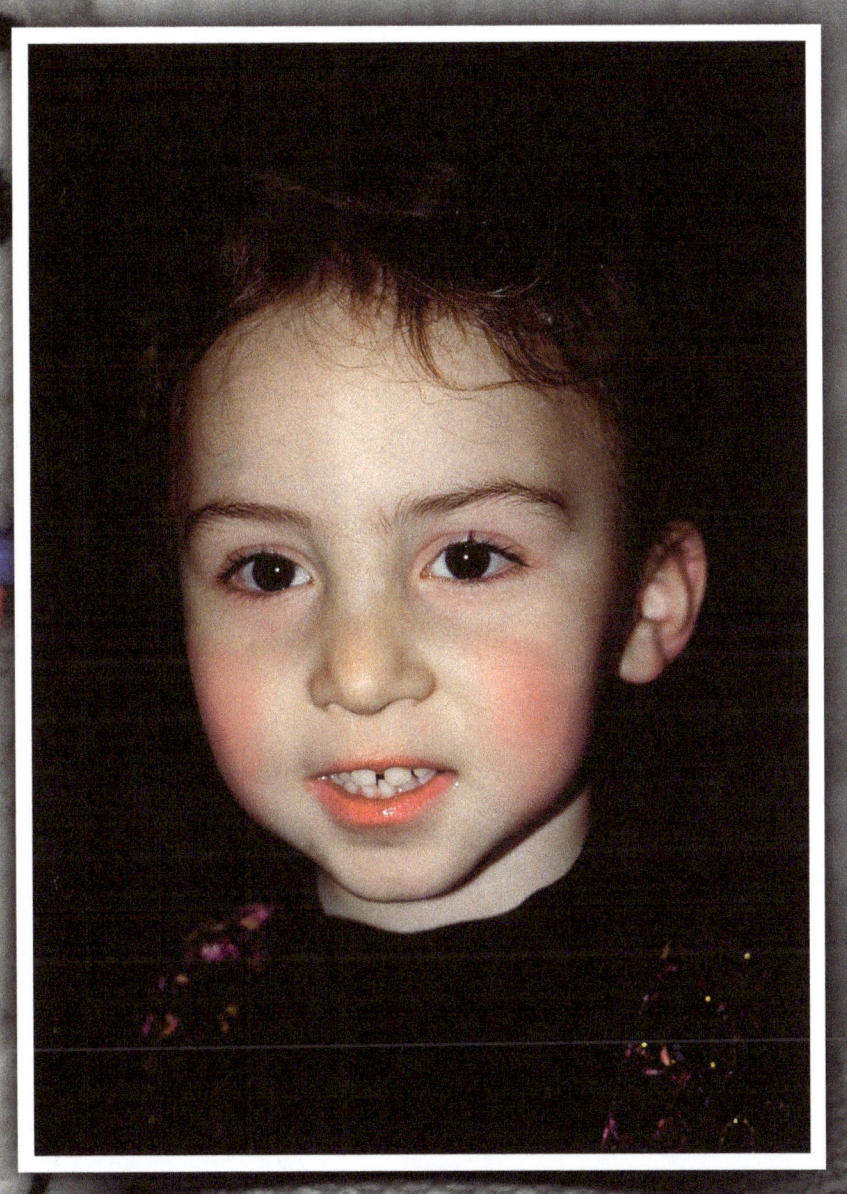

Always keep your fingers on the outside of your nose

Always keep your fingers on the outside of your nose

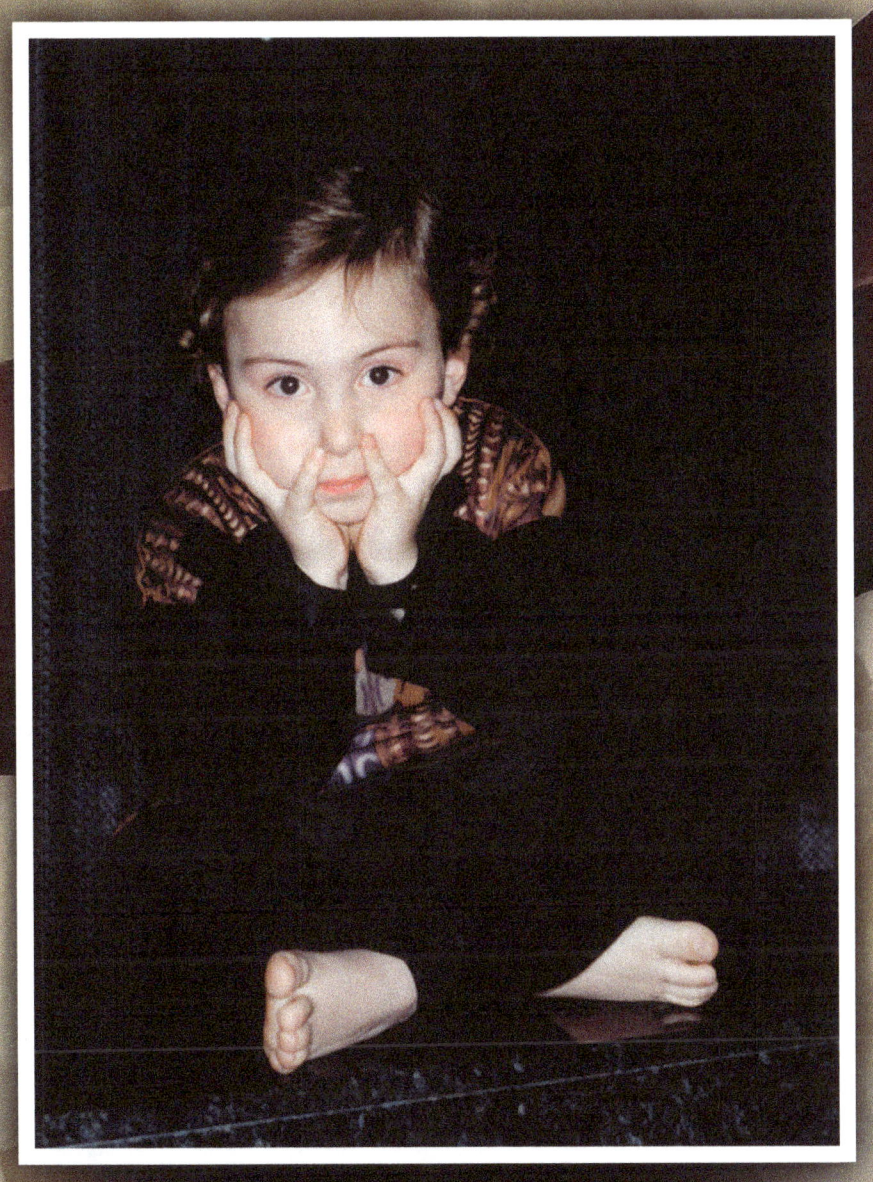

If there is something you are not sure about

If there is something you are not sure about

And someone or something makes you feel not right inside be sure to tell a grown up right away

And someone or something makes you feel not right inside be sure to tell a grown up right away

Wind and thunder
from down under
should be done
in private

Wind and thunder
from down under
should be done
in private

I'm sorry
it was an
accident

I'm sorry
it was an
accident

It's fun learning
how to
bake cookies

It's fun learning
how to
bake cookies

Make sure
you mix all of the
ingredients together
really good

Make sure
you mix all of the
ingredients together
really good

And always remember
to wash your hands
before
you start

And always remember
to wash your hands
before
you start

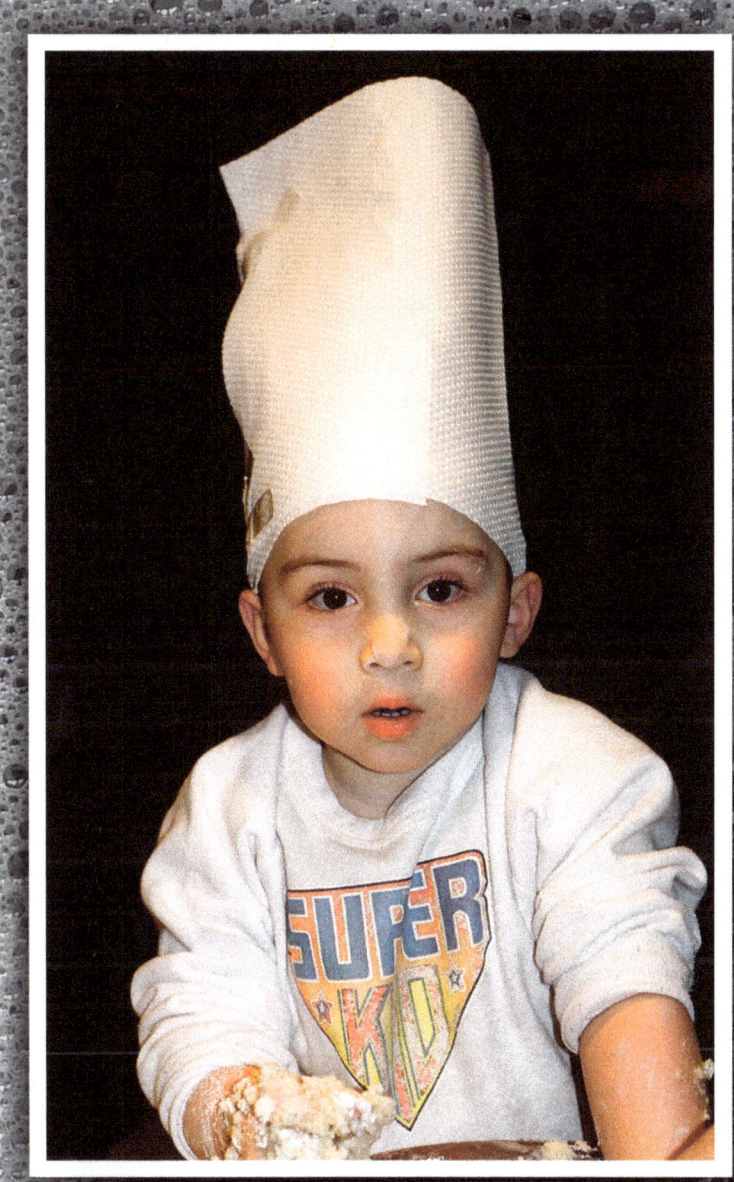

When a friend
needs someone
to talk to

When a friend
needs someone
to talk to

Always try
to be a
good listener

Always try
to be a
good listener

Never never
ever ever
eat
yellow snow

Never never
ever ever
eat
yellow snow

Sometimes
people tell stories
that are not true

Sometimes
people tell stories
that are not true

Make sure you tell stories that are true

Make sure you tell stories that are true

It's fun to feel the
wind blow through
your hair

It's fun to feel the
wind blow through
your hair

and the sand wiggle
between your toes

and the sand wiggle
between your toes

55

Being nice makes
all kinds of
friends

Being nice makes
all kinds of
friends

When you sing,
sing with all
your heart

When you sing,
Sing with all
your heart

Whenever you get
the chance
just dance

Whenever you get
the chance
just dance

Always take the
time to stop
and smell the flowers

Always take the
time to stop
and smell the flowers

Thank you for reading my
little book and letting me
share some of my real
life lessons with you
by Chance

Thank you for reading my
little book and letting me
share some of my real
life lessons with you
by Chance

This is the first book of the Learn by Chance series.

www.learnbychancebooks.com

About the Author

Gail Daldy was born in Chilliwack, British Columbia on the west coast of Canada before settling on Bowen Island which is just off the Vancouver mainland. As a young woman she travelled extensively experiencing different cultures and everyday living in numerous countries.

From this she realized children are similar the world over and can learn from each other and the simple things that surround them. She believes this collection of chance photographs captures many of these everyday life lessons and illustrates them in an easy to understand way.

www.ingramcontent.com/pod-product-compliance
Lightning Source LLC
Chambersburg PA
CBHW061930290426
44113CB00024B/2865